Marygrove
EX LIBRIS

PROFILE OF SALAZAR

MATERIAL FOR THE HISTORY OF HIS LIFE AND TIMES

PROFILE
OF SALAZAR

MATERIAL FOR THE HISTORY
OF HIS LIFE AND TIMES

BY
LUIZ TEIXEIRA

SPN
BOOKS
LISBON

Sociedade ASTÓRIA, Ld.ª — Regueirão dos Anjos, 68/70 — Lisboa

There are men who rise through their own initiative and men who are raised in spite of themselves. But any man whose intellectual ability is outstanding in the high position he has achieved or has been placed in must inevitably have begun by finding out for himself his superiority over his fellows. Society has so much to do and likes work so little, that it has little time or little inclination to go in search of unknown genius.

... ...

I don't know whether I haven't something of partiality in my judgement, which complete unanimity of opinion necessarily creates, but I admire that man...

(From the collection of incomplete manuscripts of King D. Pedro V — Reference to Mousinho da Silveira).

POOR, A POOR MAN'S SON(¹)

On the hill can be seen the houses of Santa Comba overlooking the
fertie and pleassantly wooded valley of the river Dão. Rising above
a broad dark patch of orchard trees, the graceful towers of the
church stand out against the sky. Their bells are merrily ringing
on this Sunday in May, while a religious procession descends the
street, known as Calçada Velha. It will be joined by others from
the neighbouring hamlets, and all are on their way to the shrine
of Santa Cruz do Vimieiro. Banners waving aloft, scarlet cloaks
of guildsmen, spreading canopies, statues of saints borne slowly
along on flower-strewn litters, and charming children with glowing
cheeks — then band playing solemn music with a well marked rhy-
thm, and finally at the back all the people of the surrounding
parishes in a silent and straggling cortège.

People from *Rojão*, from *Casal Novo* and other districts have all come
to watch the simple and ingenuous ceremony of the *Encontro*.
As soon as the religious rites are over, they stroll anary into the
fair. There, amid fishing-nets, onion-heads, sweet-meats and trin-
kets, bright splashes of colour lure them towards the baskets of
luxuriant oranges from *Besteiros*.

Vimieiro on the morrow returns to its peaceful everyday existence.

On one side the majestic profile of the *Estrêla* range, and on the
other, but closer at hanl, the massipe outline of the *Caramulo*
mountains. Life in these surroundings is a sweet idyll with nature.
The river flows among great boulders of brown granite. Along its
high banks, crowned with an uneven fringe of tranquil pines,
the olive-groves descend in symmetrical plantations, broken capri-

7

ciously here and there by hillocks where the soil, terraced firmly upon walls and caressed by murmuring streams, takes on the freshness and luxuriance of a garden.

In July of 1882, the bishop of *Coimbra* visits the place. The opening of the *Beira Alta* railway has been fixed for the following month... We must now pass over fourtenn years to the days when João Mendes used to drive his coach to the station of *Santa Comba* with curtains flying in the wind as the heavy load of luggage and passengers rattled along behind his two pairs of horses amid a cloud of dust and a clatter of bells. By this time, a new district had already sprung uf under the stimulus of the railway and presented a gleaming white cluster of little low houses. In one of these, at a bend in the road in front of the viaduct, you might often see a group of children: four girls and a boy. The former were between the ages of ten and fourteen; their brother was scarcely seven Every day they used to walk to the town. The girls went to Miss Isabel's a lady who ad once been employed in the manor house of the Baron of Santa Comba, and who now tanght needlework; he to Senhor José Duarte whose task it was to instruct the son of António de Oliveira in his first letters.

The newspapers would arrive from Lisbon, and in that year of grace, 1896, the kindly tutor must surely have led hist small pupil's quick and intelligent eye to the name of Mousinho, the man whose heroic exploits were then rousing the country to high enthusiasm.

The creation of a school in *Vimieiro* put an end to the children's daily walk to the town. Senhor José Duarte's pupil had now not far to go for his lessons, but a few yards from his home. That home was shared by humble parents, a family of the people. The father who owned this tiny dwelling was employed as steward on an estate. His wife, a woman of great intelligence, looked after the happy band of children with the utmost affection. Her name was Maria do Resgate.

The local school, however, closed down owing to the ill health of the master. Already the boy had revealed unmistakeably the qualities of a scholar, and his firts contact with books and awakened within him a delightful world of emotions which he was anxious to explore further. The problem of his education was solvel with the help of Father João Pimentel who took him into his house at *Viseu.*

The examinations for the second grade were held at the city school on August Ilth, 1899. The decisions of the examining board were posted up in the afternoon. Heading the list was a very unusual mark: 14. Against it, the name of a boy aged ten: António de Oliveira Salazar.

«... I AM INDEBTED TO THAT HOUSE FOR A GREAT PART OF MY EDUCATION, WHICH, UNDER OTHER CIRCUMSTANCES, I SHOULD NOT HAVE ENJOYED(2)»

The nineteenth century closed in a stifling atmosphere of theory and rhetoric. Violent and wide-spread efforts to adapt man,s mental outlook to the changing forces of progress had left the world in a state of exhaustion. New doctrines geat against it like waves of the sea, rudely dispelling its old romantic illusions and hurrying it on into a chaotic whirlpool of contradictory ideas. On the threshold of the new era, the world was envelopped in a confusion of prophesies all eagerly seeking fulfilment.

Nietzche, with the cries and visions of insanity, lay on his deathbed. Croce was commenting on the historic and economic faterialism of Marxist philosophy. There was a new professor at the Collège de France called Bergson. Bismarck had recently died after abanlonning «the spirit and method of the Florentine secretary» and completely reforming his ideas.

An old man of four score years and ten, pale, a halo of whte hair encircling his vast forehead from under a skull-cap, with a kindly smile and eyes penetrating, firm, yet tender — Pope Leon XIII beheld the passing of his former adversary in the religious wars of the Kulturkampf. But a little while and they would meet together in Heaven where the «iron chancellor» would have forgotten the ideological campaign of 78. Meanwhile «the worker's Pope» continued to show a perfect understanding of the needs of modern society. His messages on political supremacy, the constitution of

11

states, human liberty, the duties of a Christian citizen and the conditon of the workers addressed themselves to the uneasy conscence of the world. They cut directly across the manifestoes of the new revolutionaries who were bent on conquering horizons which the false dawn of 89 had not revealed. Leon XIII prescribled neo-Thomism. The philosophy of the *Summa* remained the exact expression of Catholic doctrine. The Church defined in trenchant terms, cleary and completely, her Christian conception of society.

The violent theorists of socialism and the apostles of collectivism, orators at international congresses speaking agains economic liberalism, builders of systems based on the destructive principle of class-warfare, these were not alone in their condemnation of the capitalist regime.

Leon XIII, in the name of the Church, also proclaimed the necessity of satisfying the legitimate social claims of the working classes. His language, his methods, his principles and solutions were, however, different.

Rome admitted the legitimacy of private property; refused to countenance, on the other hand, the defencelessness of the proletariat in an unjust social order which permited the enrichment of a few through the impoverishment of the great majority. She preached a return to Christian practice on the part of employers and salaried persons. She advocated, in conformity with this change of heart, the organisation of professions and a legislation of labour such as to enhance the dignity of the worker and to enable him to fulfil his duties as citizen, Christian and parent.

The remarkable encyclicals keenly interested the world. The movement of Catholic social action gathered strenght and energy and sounder foundations.

It was precisely i the first year of the twentieth century that the former pupil of the *Vimieiro* school entered the seminary of *Viseu*, a vast edifce, once a convent of the order of St Philip Nery, with an imposing and severe façade rising on the south side of the *Alves Martins* Gardens.

There, for eight years, his mind was formed and disciplined. His exemplary conduct, his devotion to learning, his evident intellectual vigour marked him out clearly for the course to which he belonged. Methodical and sternly self-disciprined by nature, orderly in his choice of study, he invariably revealed in the examinations a knowledge at once profound and assured. From the first his natural bent was for meticulous research, for mastering thoroughly each subject presented to his mind whether by curiosity or in the course of his duty as a student.

One of his old schoolfellows at this college thus recalls him:

«No useless sentence and still less no doubtful one ever fell rom his lips. He hid his great intellectual ability behind his great modesty, which bordered upon timidity.»

Very loyal and self-sacrificing, he was beloved by his companions and was always first in his final exafinations.

At *Vimieiro*, during the holidays, passers-by on the road to *Ovoa*, where it curves alongside the little property of António de Oliveira, would see beneath the oak on the hillside or in the little arbour behind the school a solitary figure continually reading: the student, Salazar. He might well have repeated Frederick Ozanan's phrase to describe the life he then led: «growing up in the shade and studying in solitude».

The voice of Leon XIII had gone forth into all parts of the earth. The enormous personality of the *Angelic Doctor* had risen again from the Middle Ages with renewed prestinge and authority.

The encyclicals were, in so many individual cases, to influence human destiny, shaping future paths for men to follow, affording instruction and guidance which time would consecrate into systems and axioms of universal interest. They are the modern expression of the social doctrine and the philosophy of the Church, seeking to reorganise society.

13

The theological course which Salazar began to prepare for in 1900 was, naturally, coloured by the ideas of the great humanist.

In 1908, the student António de Oliveira Salazar finished his studies at the seminary. Some of his companions were afterwards to join the advance guard of political democracy. He, while abandoning an ecclesiastical career, had already moulded the principal lineaments of his personality and character. His brilliant intellectual life was based on exceptionally solid foundations.

«AT THAT TIME, I WAS WORKING IN A COLLEGE WHICH ATTEMPTED TO ADAPT THE METHODS AND AIMS OF ENGLISH EDUCATION TO PORTUGAL» (³)

Nineteen hundred and eight. He was still in *Viseu*. Salazar was ninetten years old. *Coimbra,* the ancient university of Portugal, was now the engrossing object of his ambitions, luring him to a further pursuit of knowledge and to conduct his studies on a more comprehensive scale. These thoughts dictated all his plans for the future, became «the be all and the end all» of his life, which was beginning to take outward shape. He entered the *Via Sacra* College as prefect of studies. Its director, Canon Barreiros, was attempting to establish in our country the educational methods of typical British schools. A similar experiment had already appeared in France and was being carried out at the *Ecole des Roches* by E. Demolins.

Meanwhile Salazar read *La Science Sociale;* he analised the differing socail outlooks of those who were in favour of private schools and those who believed in community schools; and he became convinced that the recognised superiority of the Anglo-Saxon race was due to certain fundamental principles inherent in their education. He was persuaded that «by means of educational procedure these principles could be grafted onto the tender minds of children». This idea took possession of the young man. «It would perhaps be possible to implant the requisite good habits of thought and to create the right atmosphere, so that at least something of our educational effort might take root. Then, the little men we were

15

training for life would themselves became, later on, educators of new generations» (⁴). The national problema was really an educational problema: «it was, therefore, of small value to change governments and regimes, if you didn't first of all attempt to change men themselves. What was needed was 'men', and they had to be created by means of education. So I then began to study pedagogy. I read a number of books on education — cristicisms of old-fashioned methods, extravagant eulogies of modern ones, new points of view, new objects to achieve in the education of boys. And out of all this I gained at least one solid conviction: that, officially, in our country, «education» in the sense of an integral and harmonius development of all the individual faculties did not exist. The State undertook almost exclusively intellectual education» (⁵).

When you looked into the matter, all it amounted to was — «a little learning».

«I LIVED ABSORBED IN MY IDEA AND MY
WORK. ONLY THOSE WHOSE LIVES ARE
FILLED WITH A GREAT THOUGHT OR A
GREAT AFFECTION CAN .POSSIBLY UNDERS-
TAND WHAT THIS MEANS. IN SHORT, I
WAS A BOY WITH A SERIOUS IDEA» (⁶)

He spent the years 1908 — 1909 in the performance of his duties at
the college. He also sat for two examinations in order to complete
his lyceum course — 17 marks.

To take this course, he had had to attend an establishment of secondary
education. He was now invited to give a talk to the pupils there.
So he gave them an outline of his ideas on «education», pointed
out the deficiencies in the usual Portuguese training and put forward his views as to the system to be adopted.

Dr. Côrte Real, Dr. Barata and Dr. Rocha presiding. It was December
Ist, 1909: Restoration Day. Saladar was twenty years old. Tall
and thin, dressed in black, with a calm but piercing gaze, he
began by saying: «Fortunately, I have not been asked to make
a regular speech!». And further on he said: «... nature has not
endowed me with much gift for public speaking».

Those were the turbulent days of Republican propaganda. Days of
endless speech-making, in assemblies, in clubs, in the Parliament
of São Bento. But Salazar, without the least reference to this
fact, emphasised that «something more practical is needed at the
present historic moment». His whole lecture is an important document. It is a detailed study of education and teaching, remarkably

17

original in its handling of current problems, and displaying already a high individuality in the style and clarity of its argument.

«It is a great task to mould a human soul! It is indeed a mighty task to form a character, an individual — body, mind and will — an individual such as this poor Land of Portugal needs in order to be great».

There is a prophetic ring in this and other passages of the address. «It is ideas that govern and direct the destinies of peoples, and it is great men who have great ideas. And we, we have no men. We have no men because we have not trained them, because we have never concerned ourselves with educational method».

And he proceeds: «... We who are the Portugal of tomorrow, we who will became her deputies, her ministers, her civil servants; her lawyers, doctors and teachers, we who are now at school and will one day constitute the governing and intellectual element oh this our country, we who perhaps have already written our newspaper-article upon her embarrassed finances or the scandal of her internal politics, what are we doing to promote the prosperity of our native Portugal?».

Then follows a dispassionate criticism of hedonism, of inertia, and of work without enthusiasm. He alludes to the influence of local environment upon the character of a people. He appeals for a general reform. «But we are the nation of reforms», he cries, «and each time our position is worse! Everything has been reformed except that which must in reality be attended to first: — men!».

He goes on to suggest a return to the old conception of the family as the sphere of education. «To be a father, to be not only a father but a good father, that is the educator's prime aspiration».

«NOTHING GREAT CAN BE ACHIEVED WITHOUT FAITH» [7]

In an age distraught with verbiage and flights of rhetoric, this twenty-
-year-old boy set a solemn example. He displayed a a sense of
duty at once strong and enlightened by an accurate awareness
of indisputable facts. He was impartial in his critical commentary,
brilliant in analysis, expressed himself perfectly, was meticulous
and controlled in assessing problems and in putting forward solutions. The closing words of his lecture have a lofty glow of
national feeling: — «It is needful for the Portuguese of today to
create in the young the glorious Portugal of tomorrow — a strong
Portugal, an educated Portugal, a moral Portugal, a hardworking
and progressive Portugal Is it necessary for the fulfilment of this
purpose that we love our country deeply? Oh, it is always
necessary to love one's country, and, just as we love our own
mothers deeply, so let us also love our country, the great mother
of us all».

The student António de Oliveira Salazar was indeed «a boy with
a serious idea».

Before leaving for the University, the prefect of studies at the *Via
Sacra* College was to speak for the second time at *Viseu*. They
were not crowds of electors who listened to him. He addressed
himself simply to parents, to all those for whom the education
of their children was a serious and persistent preoccupation. Politics
were left out of the question. They were no part of the speaker's
intention nor of his words. He spoke about the development of
the spirit of initiative, about the pernicious tendency to restrict

19

education to vocational training, about the high dignity of independent labour. He refered to those «decadent pessimists who darken with their prophecies of death our hopes for the regeneration and agrandisement of our country». And, with perfect seriousness and dispassionate vision, he defended notwithstanding his exact comprehension of existing circumstances and his awareness of the gravity of the problems and the number of the obstacles to be overcome — he defended» a little optimism needful for the proper success of a great undertaking» [8].

«I CAME TO COIMBRA IN OCTOBER OF 1910, SHORTLY AFTER THE PROCLAMATION OF THE PORTUGUESE REPUBLIC...» [9]

In a state of bewilderment and delirium, the country abandoned its constitutional Monarchy and pluged violently into a democratic Republic. Twenty years of opposition, more or less tolerated, had created martyrs for the hostile party, had revealed its valuable men, had painted an attractive mirage of political principles, programmes and new horizons. On all sides and in every department of the nation's life, there was evident weariness of the political scene hitherto, of the two political parties rising alternately to power in monotonous and comfortable rotation. At the same time, an ever increasing distrust was felt for the half-hearted royalists, engrossed as they were in the suicidal madness of inter-party quarrels.

Hintze, in the exaggerated phrase of a Lisbon newspaper on the day of his death, had been «the last monarchist» [10].

The Republic, equipped with a valuable group of thinkers and economists, was proclaimed as the timely intervention of a redeeming hand and as a formula of salvaton. It was accordingly received with all the transports and mystic enthusiasm of an ideal. It arose as the logical outcome of a need created and nourished in men's hearts and minds by a long course of deeply-moving, open-air propaganda.

The new régime became a *fait accompli* ratified by law, and an occasion for festivities.

21

To set the Republic on its feet, that was to be the main preoccupation of the historical period now inaugurated.

Later on, however, a further and complementary task would be entailed: that of consolidating the Republic until it grew to be accepted almost unanimously as a national reality.

The firts of these two tasks fell to the Propaganda men, men who were soon to be became involved in a crowd of ambitious upstarts.

When, in what circumstances and to whom would be entrusted the second mission — to whom would it be given to consolidate the new régime, to endow it with the dignity and prestige proper to a great undertaking, to plant it outside the passions of party dissension and where, secure in its work of national regeneration, it would be guided only by the highest awareness of the true interests of the nation?

«I AM NOT INDIFERENT TO THE POLITICS OF MY COUNTRY: ON THE CONTARY. BUT I AM CONVINCED THAT POLITICS ALONE ARE INCAPABLE OF SOLVING THE GREAT PROBLEMS NOW WEIGHING UPON US, AND THAT IT IS A SERIOUS ERROR TO PIN ALL OUR HOPES UPON THEIR DEVELOPMENT OR UPON ARBITRARY CHANGES IN THEIR NORMAL PROCEDURE»

....

«THE SOLUTION TO OUR TROUBLES LIES WITHIN EACH ONE OF US, RATHER THAN IN THE POLITICAL COLOUR OF OUR MINISTERS» [11]

In that month of October, after the Revolution, the first man to be president of the republican municipality of *Coimbra* was Sidónio Pais. Echoes of the fall of the throne had reached the ancient University city with its solemn traditions and its immemorial practice a few days after the revolutionary scenes in the Rotunda in Lisbon.

The cloisters of the University were thrown into confusion and the cry of revolt raised. The students broke into the lecture-halls, and in an access of riotous folly destroyed the rostrums. The robes of the Professors of Theology lay torn in pieces on the floor. In the *Sala dos Capelos,* the portraits of former kings of Portugal were riddled with bullets and slashed with knives.

In 1891, João Chagas, after witnessing through his prison bars the

23

revolutionary events of January in that year, made the following entry in his notes for his chapter of reminiscences entitled «*Alvorada na História*»: — «In a neighbouring smithy the hammer, regardless of what was happening outside, continued to hammer».

In 1910, the pamphleteer did well to refrain from calling attention to the indifference of the working classes. It would, however, have been worth his while to have noted and recorded for posterity the case of that new student of the Faculty of Law, who had just passed his Lyceum-examinations in *Viseu* and who now, in his modest lodgings on the hill, was quietly waiting, amid the disturbances, for calm and serenity to be restored within the Iron Gates of the University over the way.

The new rector arrived. He was one of the great figures of the republican regime. Many years had passed since he had last crossed the *Via Latina* — a black-gowned student with a kind and open gaze, fair hair and a romantic soul. But he still possessed the same simple and ingenuous spirit, he was still at heart a dreaming, ingenuous poet with all the idealism of an early apostle. Unbalanced by the course of events, this man who had formerly preached God, though in hymns of praise for the new creed, now on becoming rector declared that «the work of harmony will be achieved without God or king». At the same time he announced the free courses and the abolition of the Theologic al Faculty and religious pledges.

Under the judas-trees in the Botanical Gardens, two poets — Engénio de Castro and António Sardinha — recalled the literary festivals of *Salamanca*. Perhaps, already with some regret, they repeated the verses of the *Lírica de Outubro*.

A few short years later, and the second of these men, together with others, was to obey his feeling for tradition and turn his back on the Republic. Meanwhile Arriaga had exchanged his rectorial chair for the President's *fauteuil* — and for all the bitternes and disillusionment that he was to find there.

24

From 1910 to 1914, the student António de Oliveira Salazar followed
the course of the Faculty of Letters. Studying under Marnoco e
Sousa, he became an outstanding figure in the University, its most
brilliant and distinguished pupil. He was held in particular respect
by his companions, was esteemed and valued by his teachers.
In November of 1914, the congregation of the Faculty met to
appraise his merit — he obtained his bacharel degree with 19 marks.

He took no part in the joyous supper-parties at the *Cardosa* nor in
the gay conversation groups held in the bookshops of the lower
town, To make his stay at *Coimbra* possible, he had to spend
some of the hours he would otherwise have devoted to study in
giving private tuition. By this means he secured the bare margin
of assistance sufficient to pay matriculation — fees and board and
lodging in the city. All the while, he was living in a restless,
turbulent atmosphere of political passions. He was present at the
explosion of public disturbances. He had entered the Iron Gates
of the University, one of a generation which was destined perhaps
to supplant in the various departments of Portuguese life the
worn-out apostles of «progress» and the opportunists who had
so rapidly passed from one régime to another, ready to sacrifice
their real convictions and to adapt themselves to circumstances in
order to achieve success.

Was he, all this while, indifferent to the unrest, aloof from the turmoil,
unmindful of forming his own political and spiritual beliefs?

The solid moral structure of the man guards him from any facile
contagion. He was this preserved from the furnace of inflammable
ideas that consumed the young men of Coimbra, who fell an easy
prey to every impetuous and generous aspiration.

Like Ramalho, he was to became an ardent supporter of educated and
enlightened authority. Like him, too, he was to believe that politics
must always be guided by the necessity of bringing economic
interests into line with moral interests, by the necessity of making
the interests of each individual citizen conform as far as possible

25

with the interests of the whole community. His opinions were know to only a few of his closest friends. Nevertheless, the student Salazar, almost from his first arrival at *Coimbra*, belonged to a political club. His voice was heard at meetings, making speeches or taking part in debates; his name was signed to articles in the newspapers.

C. A. D. C. (Academic Center of Christian Democracy) was the name of the Center, whose device was «Faith, Study and Action».

A good number of the generation which later assumed Power would take over from the organisation doctrinary influence for education.

That is why some explanations about C. A. D. C. may be read in the next pages.

THE CENTRO ACADÉMICO DE DEMOCRACIA CRISTÃ

An almost forgotten name: António Francisco Cordeiro. In 1901, shortly after the April incident in which 'D. António Barroso was hooted in the *Sala dos Capelos*, when the Calmon question was at its height and the onslaught of religious persecution in full swing, he it was who gathered together half a dozen students in the convent of Santa Clara secretly and by night, and thus founded an association of university men united by intellectual affinities and by their acknowledged Catholic convictions.

It was known first as the *Centro Nacional Académico*, but to avoid any possible confusion politically with the nationalist party of Jacinto Cândido it soon afterwards came to be called the *Centro Académico de Democracia Cristã*, a name which it has kept ever since. It was destined to have a belligerent career, to fulfil an apostolic mission in the conflict of ideas and feelings, and thereby to win great moral and spiritual victories. It became — what it was always to be — a body full of vitality, enterprising, alert, dynamic, strong in moral courage, rather revolutionary and always young. Fully conscious of its high purpose, it devoted itself to the task of educating the human will, of forming men's characters in the light of the Christian ideal.

Four years after its foundation, the C. A. D. C. began to speak through its own periodical, *Estudos Sociais*, which flourished until 1910. The wonderful lucidity with which *Rerum Novarum* had revealed the pristine vigour of Catholic social teaching was reflected in its pages. The doctrines of the encyclical were studied and

27

propaganted with the utmost enthusiasm. The term *corporation* took on a new and living significance: it had acquired an exact definition in the movement to defend «the dignity and interests of the human person». At the beginning of 1912 the weekly paper, *Imparcial*, took the place of *Estudos Sociais* as the monthpiece of the Catholic cause among the university youth. This magazine had great intellectual prominence. The name of its director on the cover, a name that enjoyed the highest prestige in academic, circles, was Manuel Gonçalves Cerejeira, the ardent leading spirit in the campaign to defend the doctrines of the Church.

The editor was Francisco Veloso and his offices were in the *Rua dos Penedos* at Carneiro de Mesquita's house.

Very early in the life of this paper, a student who was at that time almost unknown, wearing a long black gown thrown simply over his narrow shoulders, mounted the staircase and submitted for publication an article on the fundamental problem of education. It was signed with a pseudonym — Alves da Silva. The real name of the author was Oliveira Salazar. Further articles appeared, all written with the same perfection of balance and style, dealing with the same theme and ending with the same pseudonym. Not long afterwards, however, their author was at Cerejeira's side, having became one of the dominant and most respected leaders of the Catholic movement for university students.

Four months after the founding of the Republic, the offices of the C. A. D. C. were attacked and its papers burnt in the street among scenes of uproar. After May of 1912 it came under new management.

Salazar, in his third year at the Faculty of Law, was the first secretary of the directing staff. When the offices reopened in December of that year, one of the speakers at the inaugural ceremony was the former prefect of the *Via Sacra* College. It was an intensely active period of his career: his views on social subjects were taking concrete shape, the extraordinary qualities of his mind

28

were beginning to be revealed, his critical faculty and standpoint were developing, his mode of thought which had already been discernible before his arrival at the university now gained precise definition and reached out to embrace larger conceptions, though without abandoning any of the fundamental assentials he had always held. The direct line of his thought and character, firm and exact from the days of is first initiatory studies in Viseu, had never once been broken by doubts or sudden deviations. The track had considerably broadened, but nothing had ever turned it from its steadfast and consistent course.

From its very foundation the C. A. D. C. was engaged activities not always clearly understood by excited spectators amid the confusion of anti-clericalism and the Republic. Outside the stream and influence of politics and party, fighting independently against what it considered the errors and prejudices of the age, it set out to train and educate along Catholic lines the new generations of university students. Strong in faith and unwavering in courage, it possessed a body of principles which it did not hesitate to publish abroad. Fired with idealism, it remained indifferent to political régimes, and during the monarchy it refused to accept the title of «royal», though requested to do so, and to add the royal crown to its crest. During the early days of the Republic it was attacked not only by the forces of the left but also by those of the right, and these latter consisted, beside the monarchists who disagreed with the social formula of the Church, of such of the older clergy who had adapted themselves to the bureaucratic situation and of the great Catholic section for whom the religious question was inseparable from a triumphant restoration of the king.

Its device: «Church and Nation outside and above régime and parties» had sometimes to be vigorously defended in the streets against the hosts of incomprehension and factious sectarianism.

At the meetings of the club, in speeches accompanied by free and lively discussion in which some of the greatest personalities of Portuguese political life today found their first opportunity to try their eoquence and powers of argument, the ideas then preoccupying the world were continually analized and criticized. On the 30th of November, 1908, Maurras and Valois were already being discussed.

As the years went on, the club studiously kept pace with the chancing outlook of the age, which came increasingly to be characterized by its absorption in «social» and «economic» problems. When finally in 1931, *Quadragesimo anno*, the encyclica of Pius XI appeared, the Pope's message was not received with. exaggerated feelings of excitement and surprise. The unwearying studies of former and present members of the club, their knowledge and outlook alwaps abreast of the changes wrought by time, (which since the beginning of the centurp seems to have moved with ever swifter and more anvious steps) had prepared them to accept both logically and with conviction that admirable postscript to *Rerum Novarum*.

«I WAS MUCH STRUCK AT TIME BY THE ANTI-RELIGIOUS FORM WICH DEMOCRACY HAD TAKEN IN THE LATIN WORLD» ([12]).

The student members of the C. A. D. C. completed their courses, left Coimbra behind and carried away with them into all parts of the Country the spirit of their cultural reunions at the club-which, be it said, had allowed them from the very beginning entire liberty to choose their own opinions or political theories.

The Catholic Youth movement now made its appearance, attracting boys of all classes and conditions.

In May of 1914, Oliveira Salazar, in his fifth year at theFaculty of Law, repeated a lecture in Oporto which he had recently given in Viseu on the theme: «Democracy an the Church».

A report in an Oporto newspaper of the time says: — «It is long since the platforms of our assembly-rooms have been occupied by an orator so distinguished and impeccable in style, so sublime and uplifting in his ideas. His is a great intelligence, one of the most powerful minds of the new generation». The lecture develops these three fundamental ideas: «The secondary importance of forms of government Democracy as an historical fact, an irresistible trend, a legitimate conquest, is perfectly compatible with catholicism. The need to mould democracy along the lines of the programme presented by Toqueville himself: — 'to instruct it, regulate its movements ond adapt its government according to different times and places».

One sentence:

— «A democracy cannot long continue if it grants privileges to one

31

class to the detriment of others. This must bear the name, demagogy, and is incompatible with the Church, with history, with politics and wiht human reason».

At the end of the session in which other orators spoke, there were riots. Outside the audience was hooted, many Catholic supporters had to be taken to the hospital, the windows of the Association's rooms were smashed by the stones of the aggressors.

To the head of the government a telegram was sent protesting against this attack upon the right to hold meetings, a boasted and sacred privilege.

In 1935, Salazar in a public reference to this episode, commented: «It was a régime of liberty!».

The members of the C. A. D. C. were soon to be found occupying chairs in the old university; or mounting the parliamentary platform at *São Bento;* or on the battle-fields of France and Africa. They still kept on their membership and meanwhile their numbers recruited from the lecture-halls continued to grow.

On the 21st of March, 1915, António Francisco Cordeiro, whom Dr. Correia Pinto, his colleague in 1901, had called the *Alma Mater* of the C. A. D. C., came to Coimbra and presided over a cultural session at the club. By his side, acting as secretaries, were Doctors Gonçalves Cerejeira and Oliveira Salazar.

In 1938 the illustrious jurist of Corporative Law was to write about this old club «that Prof. Oliveira Salazar was a member and its guiding spirit»: «his influence upon the actual doctrine and policy of Portuguese Corporativism is profound, especially in everything concerning the defence and protection of the human person». ([18])

«I HAVE GIVEN TO THE FACULTY OF LAW AT COIMBRA ALL MY INTELLECTUAL POWERS, ALL MY ENERGY, ALL MY ENTHUSIASM IN THE CAUSE OF EDUCATING SO VALUABLE A PART OF PORTUGUESE YOUTH» (14)

Completing his studies in 1914, he at once made part of the teaching staff of the University, though not until the 28th of April, 1917, and after a competitive examination, was he formally appointed to the post of assistant lecturer in the Economic Sciences group. A year later and a month before he obtained his Doctor's degree, he was made a regular professor in the same group.

In the newspaper *Liberdade*, which came out in Oporto in 1914 Prof. Oliveira Salazar published some remarkable commentaries upon Economics and Finance, taking up a clearly defined attitude and uniting economic with political criticism.

«*O ágio do ouro, sua natureza e causas (1891-1915)*», «*Questão cerealifera do Trigo*», «*Alguns aspectos da crise das subsistências*», and the articles «*Sôbre que valor incide a contribuïção de registo por título oneroso*», «*Da não retro-actividade das leis em matéria tributária*», «*A competência dos tribunais do contencioso e a simulação de valor na contribuïção de registo*», «*Tributação das emprêsas agrícolas coloniais*» in the *Boletim da Faculdade de Direito*, and on «*A moderna técnica tributária*» and «*Direito fiscal*» in the *Revista de Legislação e Jurisprudência*. These and other studies and essays all anticipate his future professorial career.

His attitude as a lecturer can be seen in the warnings with which he usually ended his lessons:

«This is my opinion. You, gentlemen, after consulting the works I have recommended to you and well weighing in your minds the arguments both pro and contra, will adopt the opinion that seems best to you.»

«It seems to me that this problem has not as yet been sufficiently studied and understood to make it possible, in he present state of the science, to form any definite opinion upon it.»

In 1918, in the opening lesson of the Political Economy course, he thus summed up his aims and system as a teacher:

«For me, as professor, nothing would be more deplorable than not to make every effort in my power, within the limits of my subject, to familiarize the minds of. my pupils with all the great facts, all the great ideas, all the great currents of opinion traversing the world and, for good or ill, directing its course. Whatever our personal opinions may be on this or that question, we ought always to keep an open mind for new facts and new ideas, in a laudable desire to progress, continually to rectipy our knowledge and revise our mental outlook.

In March of the following year a campaign was got up against the Faculty of Law at Coimbra, under pretext of overhauling the professorial staff and reorganizing the teaching on republican lines.

Four of its professors: doctors Oliveira Salazar, Carneiro Pacheco, Fezas Vital and Magalhães Colaço were suspended until the investigations into the ancient University had been concluded. The testimony of Prof. Salazar in the ensuing trial was a noble and serene examination of conscience, published later under the tile of «A minha resposta». It remains a valuable document for the study of the personality of the author.

«In view of the political nature of the motive given for my suspension, in view also of my particular attitude and habits of thought, I might easily have written excessively in self-defence, which would have been adjudged weakness of character. And I reqretted at the time that did not possess any marked political individuality», he writes in the preface to this little work.

During the investigation, his private and public life were closely examined and all his actions inquired into.

«Of the twenty-two witnesses heard (not including in this number those brought forward by the defence), only one man accuses him, the twentieth — the others either make no mention of him or else refer to him in flattering terms as regards both the tenure of his chair and his life apart from the exercise of his duties». Such is the report of the leader of the investigation concerning Prof. Oliveira Salazar, who is accused of nothing more than of having once been a colleague of his own accuser twenty years ago at a seminary for priests...

And the report concludes: «the trial reveals no complicity whatever on the part of any of the professors of the university in the recent monarchist movement, nor can it be deduced therefrom that any of these professors has committed acts that may be considered before the law as hostile to the Republic».

The University of Coimbra was not to be deprived of any of her most distinguished teachers.

A DAY IN THE CHAMBER OF DEPUTIES SEPTEMBER 2ND, 1921

In dark corners, in the shadows, somewhere already perhaps the crime was being hatched, the sinister plans were being studied, the weapons for the murder were being fingered. Possibly too in the streets the victims were already being watched by the assassins and their movements calculated. It was a month prior to the bloody scene in Arsenal, the outrage that was to cast shame upon our Country so weary of revolutionary incidents, so weakened by ineffectual government.

By the month of September, 1921, the economist Barros Queiroz was no longer in power. His farewell message to the Head of the State is well known. He considered that the government was morally bound to make «great reductions in public expenditure» if it was to «exact fresh sacrifices from the tax-payers». Finally, in a sad and moving outburst, he drew this picture of the politics of his times: «slander, lack of consideration, insults, gross rudeness and calumny have punished my caprice in aspiring to do service to my Country».

António Granjo, «builder of ideals, devotee of liberty» ([15]), was now the President of the Ministry.

The national bitterness attendant upon «a currency debased by unbalanced budgets» and upon the «continually changing governments» vanished a nightmare in the optimism of his pronouncement to Parliament.

While Leote do Rêgo in Paris commended the dissolution of parliament in the columns of *Le Temps,* the sessions continued at *São Bento.*

37

In the centre of the great hall of representatives, there were three Catholic deputies. The roll-call was taken. Among the names was heard that of António de Oliveira Salazar.

A man dressed neatly and simply in blak, with a cold and concentrated expression, rose to affirm his presence.

But never again after that date — September 2nd, 1921 — did that name answer the call in the Chamber of Deputies.

★

★   ★

Some time afterwards in Coimbra Prof. Salazar was walking with an old fellow-student of his, now a distinguished lawyer in a provincial town and known to be an active supporter of the Catholic movement.

«And how is your practice going?»

«Badly. Make very little ont of it and not enough for my needs.»

«I can say just the same about my job as professor. What I earn is barely sufficient to enable me to go and see my invalid mother on Sundays...»

«But it would be perfectly easy for a man of your worth and abilities to take an advisory post in some large concern or other, become legal advisor to a bank...»

A hard, severe, offended look came into the professor's face. Concealing perhaps other reasons connected with his moral outlook and integrity, he says with some force:

«No. I oughtn't to and haven't time... My classes alone, the preparation of my lectures take up all my working hours...»

«ALL POLITICAL POWER CLAIMING TO ACT EFFECTIVELY IN THE REAL INTERESTS OF THE NATION MUST BE BASED ON AN ORGANISATION, NOT EXCLUSIVELY POLITICAL BUT SOCIAL, OF PROFESSIONS AND CLASSES (¹⁶)

Nineteen twenty-two. The Catholic movement was imperfectly understood and frequently calumniated. The attacks came from all sides, both the left and the right. The seeds of misunderstanding had sprung up within the fold itself, fomenting divisions and disobedience. A full and exact statement of its aims was urgently needed. It was imperative now, to appeal to the consciences of those who were not yet immured in the water-tight compartments of party politics and reveal to them the true purpose of the movement, its basic principles, and the importance of studying its procedure and position.

In the April congress a man of high repute came forward; he is thirty-three years old. The sound moral structure of his thought is unassailable; the extraordinary qualities of his mind, already conspicuous, are held in deep respect; his career of study and action has given ample signs of exceptional intelligence and is remarkable, moreover, for its steadfast adherence to one guiding idea. Thus equipped, it is he who now, with all the power of logical argument and with relentless clarity, makes a definite pronouncement upon the problem.

This speech can be considered today as the first great political document of Dr. Oliveira Salazar. He defined its subject matter as follows:
—«...there is neither intolerance nor hatred here. I have simply

39

written forty pages on Portuguese politics... and I have spoken no evil of anyone».

In this work we are astonished to find the intellectual vigour of the university professor already combined with the language of the «Speeches»: the same precise and exemplary style, controlled and chaste and distinguished. We find too, and above all, athat calm and prudent vision, objective approach, firm hold on realities and impartial accuracy, which set him quite apart in type and stature from the run of public men in Portugal at that time.

I am unable in the present study to refer at length to this document. And it is a pity. For I consider it to be essential for a complete understanding of the figure whose profile I am sketching in these pages. But my purpose is simply to contribute (though with a high seriousness) to the festivities commemorating the date marked by his taking over the admnistraton of our country.

The document fixes the principles of Christian political law: — Complete liberty for Catholics to prefer, in the realm of speculation, one form of government or another and to adhere to a newly-established régime; also the strict precept of obedience, in the name of peace and the common good, to established governments and *a fortiori* to legitimate governments. He expounds the policy of the Church, its aims and foundations, its relation with the State, how Catholics can collaborate in that policy, and what is the position of the Church with regard to the policy of the Naion. To pursue a national policy independently of the Church (provided that the principles of morality are upheld) is also in itself an end not unworthy. Benedict XV recommended Portuguese Catholics to obey those in authority over them (no matter what the form of government or the civil constitution of the Country) without reserve and in whole-hearted furtherance of the common weal. The Pope, in inviting the faithful to obey the civil power in good faith, had recognized their duty to accept public responsibilities willingly and thus to unite in promoting the progress and prosperty of their native land, Salazar concludes his lucid and calm exposition in these words:

«In innumerable cases the interests of the Nation and the interests of the regime are practically inseparable.»

«A Catholic filling a responsible post in a government may not use the confidence reposed in him aganst that government, and should a clash occur in which he can either betray or defend the government, he ought, for honesty's sake, to defend it.»

He little thought then that eleven years later, as Head of the Government, he would put this trought into practice: — «When the Army invited me to take part in the Government, it paced the problem of the Nation for me above the problem of our institutions. The existing régime had therefore to be defended. I agreed, I accepted, and that is unshakably my position». (17)

The document proceeds to develop his ideas. The whole of it is a political message of the highest importance. It stresses «the uselessness of a political reform wich does not arise out of a moral reform»; it examines in detail all the preoccupations of Catholics at that moment — 1922; it establishes doctrine and touches on certain points that may be summed up in the hope that — as another contemporary thinker (18) would have expressed it — «the teachings of the Church may go hand in hand with the lessons of history».

The work develops the following theme — among others:

«We have arrived at a stage of political and social evolution in which a political party founded upon the ndividual interests of citizens or electors has no longer the right to exist. Isolated man is an abstraction — a fiction created chiefly under the dominating influence of erroneous principles current in the last century.»

«IT IS GOOD THAT IN THIS PATRIOTIC ASSEMBLY THE NEW GENERATION OF SCHOLARS FROM OUR UNIVERSITIES SHOULD COLLABORATE IN THE TASK OF FORMING OUR OPINIONS AND COORDINATING THE THOUGHT AND ASPIRATIONS OF THE VARIOUS CLASSES OF PORTUGUESE SOCIETY» (19)

A year and a half later, early in December of 1923, the Congress of the Commercial and Industrial Associations of Portugal was held in Lisbon. The session on the night of Dec. 2nd was given over to a debate on a work by the professor of Law, Dr. António de Oliveira Salazar, entitled *«Redução das despesas públicas»*. It is a plan of action, a programme of government in the economic and financial sphere — a promise of the days to come. Salazar, the technical expert, analizes our financial problem with a clarity of which the Country was only later to become fully aware, revealing the situation in all its aspects and calculating the consequences.

One of the speakers (Dr. Levy Marques da Costa), praising this work written «with elegance and brilliance», declared:

«I have long been preaching the absolute necessity of giving these young men a hearing in the discussion of our national problems; these intelligent and erudite men, working unseen in their studies, are full of patriotism and faith and will surely play a most important part in this mission of saving the Country.

«DICTATORSHIP PRESENTS ITSELF AT THIS MOMENT AS AN URGENT NECESSITY» [20]

Two weks passed. The capital was shaken by yet another revolutionary movement. The ministry fell after little more than a month of ffice, and there were violent altercations and disorderly scenes in Parliament. On the 17th, the ex-minister of Finance gave a sensational lecture in the Geographical Society upon the conditions requisite to make government possible in Portugal. To the accompaniment of continual applause, Engineer Cunha Leal eloquently criticized the political situation in plain and biting terms. He chastized the garrulity of contemporary politicians; he comment ed sharply upon the spirit of permanest and sterile discussion then reigning, the sheer decadence of traditional individualism, the weakening of the central power, the reform of «the liberal Parliament, that decrepit institution which must be transformel but not removed»; then he mentioned the man who in Italy «has made order where there was disorder» and the man who in Spain «i brilliantly repairing the errors of politicians». He stated that «the public contempt for politicians includes both republicans and momarchists without distinction», and that «power which humbles itself like a beggar, bending under the weight of social disorders, and permitting a state of confusion to reign, will lead us to yet greater misfortunes». He insisted that «there are murderers whom the authorities are unable to arrest»; that «there is no firm and determined purpose to reduce expenditure»; that «for lack of resour ces, the country's development is paralized and its full development impossible», and that for this and other reasons, which he ennume-

45

rated; «the Portuguese currency was continuously debased, while hunger and poverty invaded the homes of the workers.»

The speaker expressed his opinions at some length, and the constructive message of the lecture was made abundantly clear when he said: «Let us save the Nation by means of honest politicians backed up by the Public Security services!». «The Army ought not really to act against the politicians, but it has the right to make its voice heard and to point out to the public authorities that, if it is to avert the threatening dissolution of Portuguese society, it has the right to speak — on pain of everything, absolutely everything, being lost in Portugal».

On the following day, the newspapers published reports of the lecture. *Novidades* devoted two columns of its front page to the event, and alongside of them — was it chance or prophetic coincidence? — appeared a portrait of Dr. Oliveira Salazar with the heading, «Portugal born again» and, underneath, the caption, «an important figure in our movement of national rejuvenation».

Thus, at a critical moment, five years before he came to power, the professor of Coimbra was already being singled out not only as a financial expert, but as an eminent personality, a thinker possessing unusual mental ability and clearsightedness, one upon whom the Country could count in its sorely-needed effort of resurrection.

«THE LEGITIMATE ASPIRATIONS OF THE PRO-
LETARIAT MASSES ARE FRITTERED AWAY BY
THE FANTASTIC POLITICAL PROGRAMMES OF
THEIR LEADERS WHO FEED THE IMAGINATION
OF SIMPLE FOLK UPON IMPOSSIBLE HOPES» [21]

One day a longer book than this one will be written, giving a
detailed account of the personality of Salazar as journalist: a
most interesting and valuable chapter in his complete biography
as a public man. His articles in the daily press will be the subject of new and serious study. They are written in his own feli
citous style with a powerful logic, clarity of exposition and ideas,
sobriety and even a gentle irony enhancing the piquancy of the
criticism. But they reveal essentially the same man, the same ideas,
the same high intelligence that we know today.

A month after Cunha Leal's lecture in the Geographical Society,
Salazar published (15th and 16th of January, 1924) two articles
in *Novidades* both entitled: «*Ensino e Despesas — a questão das
Universidades*». I quote the following sentence which closes the
second of these articles, because it appears to me to sum up his
style as a political commentator «But instead of solving the question of education in the light of our national needs, we pay most
attention to purely local conveniences. Well, if, instead of reducing
our universities to only one, we are going to increase thier number
to four or five, then, if you don't mund my asking, I also would
like one... for my village.

On the 12th of March in the same year, he wrote on a to-
pical subject in connection with the debasement of the curren-

47

cy: his article was entitled: «*Arrendamentos em moeda estran-geira*».

Some months later, the First Eucharistic Congress was held at Braga. The solemm session of the 4th of July, 1924, was opened with a remarkable speech by Dr. Gonçalves Cerejeira, a professor of the University of Coimbra. There were other speakers as well, and among them Dr. Oliveira Salazar:

«The masses of the working classes whose soul rises in revolt, hunge-ring and thirsting for justice, are legion... and that legion, pro-claimed in the Gospels as blessed, passes by the Church in ignorance of Her, advances in warfare against Her — as though to destroy the source of all virtue and order in the world were the best way to conquer justice and peace».

«So then venture on movements which jeopardise modern civilisation, and, be it noted, the more they advance and the greater their gains, the more violent grows the struggle feeding on its own triumphs; and peace does not come, justice does not exist, the position remains the same, and the workers themselves see their victories crumble in their hands».

This is the real starding point of the theme which he proceeds to develop. He puts forward the concepts of the *Peace of the World and the Peace of Christ* and with skill and lucidity explains the difference between them. The former, wholly external, is achieved through *command;* the latter, wholly within, is won by *obedience.* He declares that the working classes are seeking the *Peace of the Worl,* and therefore do not achieve real peace. Next discusses the unequal distribution of wealth which is the chief characteristic of the political and economic organisation of modern peoples as a whole. He dwells upon the temptation to dominate the State and the irresistible attraction exercised by Power when it is not the fulfilment of a sacred duty, but rather a means of satistying self-interests. He speaks too of the fascination of riches when they are merely a source of self-indulgence, and not a social

·reserve or an instrument of production and wealth for the community.

Speaking of the socialists, communists, and revolutionary syndicalists, he examines the spirit which dictates their organisations — in order to bring about the *social revolution*. The latter he defines as «the taking possession of supreme Power in order to convert the interests of the workers into law; and the confiscation of existing wealth so as to bring about a new formula for the distribution of the new wealth to be created». Salazar remarks that these aims have already been achieved on certain points, and he comments: «... and peace has not come, rather the struggle has blazed more fiercely and poverty grown more bitter». And then comes a calm, impartial and profoundly critical exposure of the illusions upon LABOUR, WEALTH, and POWER which confuse and distort the mental outlook of the workers and are fatal to their true interests.

I shall now attempt to summarize Salazar's analysis of these three illusions upon which the working classes base their hopes — their dream of peace throughout the world, to be established by a redistribution of wealth and by the government being placed almost exclusively in their hands.

LABOUR: their theory, that it is only the worker who works and produces, and that the other classes of society live parasitically upon his efforts is erroneous and endangers civilization. «The hierarchy — invention, organisation, direction and executive — both fulfills an intrinsic necessity of material production, and reflects the natural inequalities between individual abilities, inequalities which society neither can nor ought to interfere with. The statesman, the judge, the lawyer, the doctor, the priest, the artist, the professor, the man of learning, are not mere ornamental flowers of a surface civilisation; they contribute to create those indispensable conditions without which production would be undeniably inferior. Order, justice, beauty, science which increases man's powers over nature and man's creative faculties, these are not material wealth; but without them production would be neither so abundant nor so valuable». Thus the idea of the exclusive or dominating importance of material labour, unaccompanied by those conditions of life which political organisation and the human spirit alone can create, such a theory is more than illusion, «it is an idea of death itself, not only for what we call our civilisation, but also for that future production of wealth which directly concerns the interests of the working classes».

WEALTH: «there is a wealth which is egoism and a wealth which is sacrifice and devotion to duty». The first kind is exclusively consumption: it satisfies natural necessities or those created artificially by civilisation. The second is that wealth which is destined to feed new enterprises of production and to increase the riches of the community: it cannot be formed without foresight and sacrifice — the sacrifice of a present appetite of consumption or the sake of some future production, and the foresight to weigh future necessities against present enjoyments.

Professor Salazar tells us that this wealth can be in the hands of private persons, of syndicates, of small local bodies, or else in the hands of the State. And pointing out that sacrifice and devotion duty require a superior type of man, he exclaims: «I can best describe this wealthy man, or rather this wealthy producer, as being like one who administrates the property of a person legally incapable of looking after it himself; one who makes the riches entrusted to him fruitful, thanks to his energy, initiative, and qualities of management and leadership.

The future Minister of Finance expresses the whole gist of his thought in these words: «What it behoves us all to do is this — not to allow the wealth we possess to rot in sterility, but to convert it into an instrument of labour, to get the utmost value from it, to fertilise it, to produce with it yet more wealth from which all may profit».

50

«Thus, in direct opposition to the first illusion of the working classes with regard to wealth, this fact emerges: that any economic or legal organisation which, by handing over all wealth to the State, leaves productive wealth within the reach of any and every appetite, will have the immediate effect of deflecting it into consumption, thus rendering it useless and diminishing it, and ultimately increasing the poverty of the whole community».

Speaking of the absence of moral or legal limits concerning the consumption or utilisation of wealth, Salazar considers this inimical to peace, since this kind of wealth never gave anyone happiness. «One desire boeeds another; the satisfaction thereof merely creates a new craving in the boundless appetite of ambition. It is like some mysterius drink, the effect of which is ever to increase our thrist».

POWER: «... to gain Power, to wield Power so that utter illusions may be transformed into actual law (which, once done, would diminish the productive capacity of the world and destroy the firm foundations of social stability), this is not to remove conflicts, it is to multiply them; it is not to seek peace, it is to incite war; it is not conquer happiness, it is to promote poverty and pain».

The whole, speech, a most remarkable piece of oratory, deserves to be published in full and distributed throughout the country. It is indeed one of the best passages in the political anthology of our times, a master-piece of objective criticism and logical argument.

He defines the mission of Christianity: «it does not need to command but to serve», «it preaches obedience te as opposed to the spirit of revolt; love as opposed to hatred, self-sacrifice as opposed to ambition». «These are the moral foundations of our social revolution». And he proceeds:

«Not to aspire to POWER as a right, but to accept it and exercise it as a duty; to consider the State as God's ministry for the common good, and to obey from the heart those who are in authority; to command without forgetting the dues of justice, and to obey without forgetting the sacred burden of those who command.

—what a tremendous social revolution this would be. It would mean Power unhampered by ambitious greed, by troublesome importunity, or by dangerous revolutions; it would mean authority free to act and the rights of the subject respected; it woul mean human law dignified by justice and Powver limited by the law of God and the rights of conscience; it would mean order ensured by obedience rooted in men's souls».

And after laying down the guiding principles which are to inform the possession of WEALTH and the exercise of LABOUR, Salazar closes with these words:

«Given that men's souls be transformed by the Christian spirit of odedience, of love and self-sacrifice, then the peace of Christ is perfectly compatible with the worker's syndicates, with new systems of labour, with new systems of property and with diferent political organisations. For the spirit will always endow them with moderation, with justice, with charity, with moral values dominating the material aspects of life».

«SOCIAL SOLIDARITY REQUIRES THAT ALL MEN SHOULD SHARE IN THE LABOUR OF THE WHOLE COMMUNITY

In April of 1925 Dr. Oliveira Salazar gives two lectures in Funchal — «*Laicismo e Liberdade*» and «*O bolchevismo e a congregação*». Both these are pieces of scientific criticism dealing with problems relating, fundamentally, to his social and economic studies. From the second of these lectures which closes with the watch word «Work, moderation and economy», we quote the following sentence:

«... theree principles which morality has long been preaching, though without effect, are now beginning to shine forth and claim the attention o the State: to wit — that social solidariy requires that all men should share in the labour of the whoe community; that what is superfluous ought not to receive attention before what is needful has been supplied; hat wealth, the combined output of human labour, ought not to be wasted, but portioned out according to the urgency of the needs it is to satisfy».

A local journalist, perhaps Feliciano Soares, reported the event, noted the didactic severity of the speaker, and, commenting on his appearance and «manner», observed with correct psychological insight: «He was addressing the public, but it was as though he were thinking aloud, as thougt he were quite alone and talking to himself» [22].

«I THOUGHT OF THIS DIFFICULT PROBLEM WHICH IS PERHAPS AN ETERNAL PROBLEM FOR STATES»

I follow Richard Bloch's footsteps in a rapid synthesis of the general European scene through the ages: — The first conception of a Europa is due to the Roman Catholic Church (in the Meddle Ages the Pope «in reality presides over an authentic League of Nations»). In the eighteeth century the spirit of the Encyclopaedists and the the French language take the place of Rome and Latin. European humanism rests definitely on a French basis. After the Revolution, during the nineteenth century, the latent hostilities explode. «Europe will shortly be nothing more than a mosaic and our minds vainly reach out in search of an impossible unity».

Then comes the War. There follows what has been called the apotheosis of Republican and democratic progress. But as soon as the conflict is over three candidates arise to dispute the succession to the old spirit of Europe: — the Roman Catholic Church, the representatives of worn-out liberal humanism, and the International Communist Party. The Totalitarian States appear and a French politician, Blum, powerless to bring bout a reaction, delivers his verdict — «Legality on holiday».

Representative democracy and parliamentarianism enter upon an extremely critical phase. Lenin, Primo de Rivera, Pilsudski, Alexander of Jugoslavia, Mussolini and even Venizelos now proceed to «dictatorship», a word which at that time was merely the name of a political phenomenon».

Barthélemy himself, the apostle of democracy, insists that our times are passionately interesting: «It is not a field of ruins; it is a shipyard where, amid the uproar of saws, trowels and hammers, a world is being constructed». And refering to 1914: «Then it could indeed be said that the future belonged to the democracies. Today we have not the same certainty».

On tre 16th lay of June, 1925, Coimbra was em fête. In the *Sala dos Capelos* the Portuguese-Spanish Congress for the Promotion of the Sciences was being held, Professor Oliveira Salazar pronounced the opening speech of the Social Sciences Session. He was thirty--five years old; his ideology, the main points of his theory, and his newly-revealed political opinions were already well-known. His speech was entitled «*Aconfessionalismo do Estado*»*. It deals with «a difficult problem, which is perhaps eternally a problem for States». He premises that society cannot live and progress without renovation and without liberty on the one hand, or subsist without order and stability in its basic organisation on the other: these two necessities — liberty and order — and these two pitfalls — disorder and tyranny — are the framework of public life in modern times. Then, with particular earnestness, Salazar asks: How far do the rights of civil defence extend? How can we afford to limit our liberties? Can somme solution to the problem be found, so that the State shall neither succumb from continual changes of its organisation and institutions, nor decay into an inert mass suffocating the renovating urge of liberty beneath the weight of its power, long after the creative life of its traditional govermnent has been exhausted? The religious unity which men fought for — explains Salazar in a reference to our past history — was not only a religious aim on the part of the State, but also ultimately a condition of peace, order and social stability. Scientific knowledge in those early days was disparaged, and art and philosophy flourished

---

* The Undenominational State.

56

under the auspices of a religious creed, which included them in its
domain: to insure religious unity was therefore to insure the unity
of the nation in the spheres of intellect and feeling. The principle
of religious liberty was later brought into force; the separation of
Church and State was achieved. «But to have a religion was not
merely to profess a creed and participate in the ritual of a cult;
it was ti possess a system from which could be derived moral rules
for individuals and principles of government for nations, because
the whole texture of religious life was ultimately based on a particular conception of social life». The divorce of religion from the
State was held to be a necessary condition for religious liberty:
such a divorce ought therefore to have been extended to any
doctrine whatever that might influence the State to adopt an
attitude or a line of action. Professor Salazar then goes on to
study in detail the results of this liberty supposedly guaranteed by
the absolute neutrality of the State. He explains that, through the
absence of any basic doctrine, the State is left to the mercy of
every current of thought, every system and suggestion that may
influence it. And not only in theory, not only in the light of reason,
but from the facts themselves, he demonstrates how far such a
system can function and how far it had actually guaranteed public
liberty.

He shows that the State cannot be organised nor act, nor defend its
members, nor defend itself except in the name of a doctrine or
through the medium of a doctrine; that it is from the realm of
philosophy itself that the State must seek the conceptions upon
which its very existence is based. He explains with detailed and
brilliant argument the impossibility of organising the State without
a definite conception of society and man, and he professes his
adhesion to a doctrine which both the discoveries of science and
the teachings of history endorse. Then Salazar proclaims: «It is
an illusion to suppose that the State has no share at all in the
absolute». And with perfect logic he adds: «We have to consider

the stipulations of the law as in truth right; to consider the verdicts of the courts as absolute justice; to hold as reasonable and right the ascendency of force. Thus we find ourselwes attributing infallibility to the decisions of a parliament, the verdicts of a court and the acts of an executive powers and at the same time admitting that violence is decreed, unjust sentences are passed and might triumphs over right».

After examining the principles upon which the Modern State is founded, and pointing out its salient and characteristic features, which, he says, are «rationalism and naturalism; individualism and liberalism; a conception of the State and a conception of the law according to an individual interpretation of society and of the will of the people», Salazar reaches his first conclusion: «No State can exist without a doctrine underlying its organisation. On the other hand States have been created with the express object of not professing any doctrine whatever; but this in itself is a doctrine, and such experiments merely disprove the claim that liberty can be guaranteed by the absolute neutrality of the State». He then proceeds to examine the functioning of the doctrineless State and to assess its practical results. «And in order that we may reach a clear and definitive conclusion, we shall do well to observe such a State in its relations with a doctrine which is diametrically opposed to its own in theory, and which would also be openly antagonistic were it able to put its theories into practice. I choose Catholicism for my example, since it exactly fits these conditions being opposed at every step to the liberalism of the modern State».

«The foundation of a State is not the *individual* but *society*: this is a natural, universal and necessary fact. *Society* consists of the family and of all those various groups which spring up and are spontaneously organised in the heart of the nation, in order to give life to man, to perpetuate his species, to defend his professional interests, assist his moral training and promote the development of his intellect. *Individual man* arises out of this society and owes his very existence to it. He is the element of which it is composed, and he, therefore, can be neither superior to it nor completely independent of it. He is an entity endowed with *liberty*, not because he always uses his liberty for good, but because without liberty the good he is capable of doing could not be brought to fruition. He is an entity neither wholly good nor wholly bad, but capable of good and evil, a being for whom virtue is the result of struggle and effort, and vice mere yielding to his strong tendencies of evil. Human institutons are not «chains» for man to break through, impediments hampering the fulfilment of his aims. They are barrier to hevagaries of his liberty, a shelter for the frailty of his nature, a sure guidance amid the hesitations of his conscience, an aid to enable him to obey the higher law imposed upon him. Since the purpose of his own existence does not lie with man, so also the laws to which he is subject are not made by him. Above him is God who created that purpose and those laws, for no moral obligation exists except it come from God, nor can any be imposed by one man upon another except in the name of God. For this reason God created the institution of power and entrusted it to those who are in command, so that the law, provided it be just and for the common good, might have the seal of its authority in its divine origin. Neither the despotism of the State nor the demagogism of the people, but rather a perfect balance between needful *authority* detached from human passions on the one hand, and *social rights* outside the sway of public opinion on the other. One notion of *society, man, liberty, law, power*, the *State*, as against another notion of *society, man, liberty, law, power*, the *State* — that is all: nothing more is needed in order to understand Christian polity.»

Then Professor Salazar shows how deeply it is in the interests of the State to impose a doctrine upon the community, and how its professed absolute neutrality has proved, contrary to its avowed intention, to be utterly at variance with the safety of human liberties. Starting from the fact that the State does not recognise the spiri-

59

tual sovereignty of the Catholic Church and therefore its rights (though it does ecognise the rights of citizens), the lecturer proceeds to discuss the ensuing infringements of religious liberty. He considers that the desire to remain in office is the strongest tendency of a self-constituted authority, and that this tendency is all the more dangerous in a Modern State which claims to found its powers not upon itself, nor its raison d'être upon a Supreme Being, but both upon the will of the people. «A variable will, continually shifting its direction, would cause the State to waver in its fundamental doctrine and in its constitution. The requisite stability can thus be obtained only in one of two ways: you must either place the Modern State outside the vagaries of public opinion — and that would be to reduce it to the very negation of all it stands for or you must keep public opinion stable in the essentials of doctrine». And Salazar asks: «why does not the State create a sound basis for itself upon *unity in the mind of the nation?* The State would then work *so to form the mind of the nation that complete adhesion is achieved to the formulated and consecrated doctrine of the State*». This means that if the State professes a doctrine, it is forced o impose it. And the speaker now describes at some length, though always with precision and critical acumen, the means employed by the Modern State to that end. Religious liberty is restricted and impiety alone is free. The system must inevitably lead eventually to the complete negation of religious liberty, since the restricted liberty a present conceded is already spoken of as tolerance in official documents. Liberty of religious association is denied, priesthood and congregation are persecuted, whenever they conflict with the social scheme, with the purity of the individualist principle and with the methods to impose its own doctrine adopted by the State. The attitude of the State ranges from allowing a quasi liberty to absolute prohibition, from sympathy and liberal condescension down to hatred and the classifying of poor friars as criminals. *Sympathy* towards missionaries, *contempt* for mystics and contemplatives, *distrust* and close *vigilance* of the charitable orders, open *hostility* and absolute *proscription* towards those who are engaged in instructing and educating the young and in forming their consciences. Nothing can be found to justify this varying attitude, says Salazar, «neither from the standpoint of the individualist principle which ought to be opposed to any form of religious association, nor from the standpoint of the principle of liberty· which ought to admit it without distinction».

He next turns to discuss *liberty in education* and the principle of the state-school, *stereotyped, undenominational* and *compulsory*. He then examines means of protecting the individual against the absorptionist tendency of the State. And finally he comments on «this unlooked-for result of individualism, whereby it hands over the individual, manacled and powerless, into the keeping of the State, and robs the child from ist family in order to educate and train it in harmony with the State doctrine and with what is supposed to be the well-being of the nation».

*

*   *

These two lectures, «*A Paz de Cristo na classe operária*» (Braga, July 4th, 1924) and «*Aconfessionalismo do Estado*» (Coimbra, June 16th. 1925) contain in their ideas, thus presented and defended, and in the reasoned faith that inspires them the basic doctrine of that ideology which was to point the way for Portugal's resurrection and ultimately to give her the new social order, the political architecture of the New State and the vigorous social sense with all its important and impressive results which she now possesses — the outcome of the Revolution, the work of Salazar, a total benefit for the country.

61

A month after the lecture at Coimbra, on the 16th July, 1925, at a
nocturnal session in the parliament of Bento, a deputy mounted
the platform and calmly announced that he intended to speak
without interruption till two o'clock in the afternoon of the following day. Actually, he finished before midday, after he had been
speaking or about nine hours.

It was the heartache of national parliamentarianism.

The next speaker was more moderate. His oratory did ot exceed four
hours...

Three days later there were dead and wounded in Lisbon, victims of
one more revolutionary outbreak.

The appeal to the army continued...

THE «NOVIDADES» CAMPAIGN

During the first quarter of the year 1928, Salazar's articles in the columns of «Novidades» followed one upon another with all the insistence of a resolute and declared campaign. In January he published «O Empréstimo externo» «Equilíbrio orçamental e estabilização monetária» and «Ainda o equilibrio e a estabilização». In the following month, «Deficit or Superavit?» and «Consignação de receitas». Under the general title of «Medidas de Finanças», he continued with his remarkable commentaries upon the situation created by Portugal's official representation at the League of Nations.

The provisional Minister of Finances, then holding office, declared in Geneva that the situation demanded the assistance of all qualified persons. On the 10th March, «Novidades» commented: «The Army, which is responsible in the present hour for the maintenance of authority, shoulders a heavy task and a patriotic mission: that of supporting and defending those who are able and competent to carry out successfully this work of financial recovery». The «competente» man was to make his appearance little more than a month later. The Army was to fulfil its patriotic mission in complete accord with the nation.

Fifteen days before he took over the Ministry of Finances he wrote: «I have long been of opinion that our social order must undergo certain reforms which time has rendered inevitable, and that, preferably, the Right Wing itself should conduct these reforms, rather than the Left be called in to do so: because violence may endanger sacred principles which, for the good of all, must never be tampered with... But we have no need to worry, for everything in this country usually turns out for the best...»

«WE IN PORTUGAL ARE FACED WITH GRAVE DIFFICULTIES, SUCH AS AROUSE OUR PATRIOTISM AND CALL UPON US TO MAKE SACRIFICES» ([23])

In march, 1928, the Catholic workers of Coimbra hold a celebration in the Ozanan Hall. At a given moment, a deep silence falls upon the room. A man who has been deputy for a day and minister for less than a week; who is a «learned professor of the University of Coimbra»; who has already been recognised as «an important figure in the movement for national revival», and is a very brilliant commentator upon the political, financial and economic events of his time; who is an educationist, and more than that — the mentor of the young «élite», mounts the platform and addressing an audience of thousands of keenly interested people hanging upon his words, begins his lecture — «Duas Economias».

It would not be long now before the Nation, aware of his abilities his exemplary honesty, his rare qualities as a thinker, his gift for statesmanship and his exceptional culture, was to ask him to take upon himself the reins of government, to play a supreme rôle which circumstances had rendered almost insuperably difficult, to accept a position which only an outstanding figure in the scale of national values could be fitted and destined to fill.

Professor Oliveira Salazar spoke in his «Duas Economias» on these two alse conceptions of wealth: — «Produce to sqcander — Produce to became the slave of money». After saying that to produce is a different thing from to earn, he developed his ideas upon the function of wealth and the value of small savings; the value of

65

saving in the home; the work of women, and the truth that it is
not only among the lower classes that homes are disorderly. He
referred to the principles laid down im the Gosples with regard to
thrift and ended with these words:

«We in Portugal are faced with grave difficulties, such as arouse
our patriotism and call upon us to make sacrifices. Patriot ism
undoubtedly lays upon us duties of various kinds, bút allow me
to give you one piece of advice: don't let us occupy our minds
with the aim, high though it be, of saving the country; let us
leave that to our rulers and to Providence. We can all do one
thing which is at once simpler and far more effective: let us
work as hard as we can — and as well as we can; in our work
and in our homes let us save and let us spend as *wisely* as we
can. The task of our rulers will be by this simple contribution
extraordinarily lightened, and they will assuredly appreciate it
more than fiery speeches. We do talk so much!»

* *

* *

The political personality of Salazar first took shape under the per-
suasive influence of the humanist Leo XIII, whose social teaching
he imbibed from the great encyclicals during the years 1900-1908.
In the two succeeding years, it began to find public expression
in the lectures at *Viseu*. A preparatory stage of expansion ensued.
It gained a higher finish in his liife with the C. A. D. C. Finally
in the Congresses of Lisbon, Braga and Coimbra and also in the
Press campaign, during the years in which he was broadening
his erudition as a University professor, his personality reached
its full fruition.

The dates and place referred to are points along the direct line of
his mental development.

«I WAS OBLIGED TO ABANDON THAT HIGH CALLING OF TEACHING AND TO TREAD A MORE DIFFICULT PATH WITH A HEAVIER CROSS» [24]

The house where Dr. Oliveira Salazar was born, where his childhood was spent, where his parents died and his unmarried sisters still live is one of the humblest dwelling in *Vimieiro*. By lifting your arm you can touch with your fingers the edge of the roof, which juts out like a pent-house roof until it is over the edge of the road. The house has a peacepul and pervading atmosphere of scrupulous orderliness. White walls, cleanliness, simplicity. Wild geraniums flower in little pots on the two stone seats at the entrance. A few steps away are two houses adjoining each other: low houses with only the ground-floor, unpretentious in design, no different from other small middle-class houses in a village. One of these is the local school, the other is the home of the President of the Council*. A creeper, loaded with clusters of flowers, unites them in gay and delicate affection.

On that Sunday in June in the year 1926, some days after the Revolution, before Gomes da Costa had yet sheathed his sword (which moreover was not stained with Portuguese blood), a motor-car filled with officials, coming from Coimbra, arrived at *Vimieiro*. Salazar received the delegates of the Revolution in his house. A few moments, he came out and walked across to his

---

* Dr. Salazar.

67

parents home. In the entrance-room were all the family, surroonding Maria do Resgate who was ill and lying back an easy-chair.

«I say, Mother, they want me to go to Lisbon to be Minister of Finance. But it is so hard for me to leave you like this... I don't know what to do...»

Dona Maria do Resgate looked lovingly at her son. A silence of deep emotion ensued. Then, resolutely, energetically, his mother replied:

«Accept. Don't think about me. If they have come here, it is because they need you. You must accept. Go, my son».

So, on the following Saturday after five days amid the scenes of public confusion, he returned to the capital, a sadder man.

The Third Congress of the Catholic Centre had been fixed for the end of April, 1928. It had been announced that Salazar would speak in it on the 27th on the theme: «The Catholic Centre and the Present Political Situation». But the Congress did not take place after all. Salazar, nevertheless, addressed Catholics on that day. And taking up the subject of his announced lecture, he spoke to them these words:

«I say to Catholics that my sacrifice gives me the right to hope that, of all Portuguese, they will be the first to make the sacrifices that I shall ask of them, and the last to ask me or favours that I shall be unable to grant them» (25).

Some hours later, on the same day, April 27 th, 1928, he formally took control of the Ministry of Finances.

Ten years passed.

In *Vimieiro*, the same tranquil, everyday simplicity reigned in the little houses of the station district. From time to time, afer lapses of many weeks, the former pupil of José Duarte would spend there a few brief days of rest. His expression is less serious when he walks among the apple-blossom up and down the paths of his little garden-property.

Lisbon is far away. Here, there are only the passers-by along the road on their way to work, the rough Beira folk who are simple and sincere. They doff their caps as they pass his door and gratefully hail the man who has given to Portugal a higher, grander and nobler nationhood.

N O T E S

We have said in the course of this work that Salazar took his examination for the certificate of primary instruction on August 11th, 1899, and passed with 14 marks. The *Revista Católica* of Viseu confirms this, but informs us that the candidate had really deserved a higher mark:

«The ten-year-old boy came to grief in his firts paper, the written paper. He was, kowever, admitted to take the oral test. This went of so brilliantly that the examiners had, perforce, to award him 18 — which in those days was a very high mark. This figure added to his written mark, 10, gives us 28, and half 28 gives us 14. But a candidate who obtains 18 marks in his oral test is obviously not likely to get only 10 for his written paper, unless he completely breaks down, which often happens of course to examinees, especially children. Had Salazar been luckier with his written paper, he would, therefore, as a child of ten — but I am not exactly sure of his age — have gained a mark of high distinction when still in the stage of primary instruction (the basis of all future education), as he was later to do in the course of his secondary and higher education where high marks are not merely *unusual* but rare. In the Seminary of Viseu he gained high marks continually; in the National Lyceum 19 or 20 marks were habitual to him; at Coimbra... everybody knows.

The most interesting part of the story was the little boy's face when he was old about 18 marks in the oral examination and his 10 in the written.

I might have got a distinction, he repeated sorrowfully.

Don't worry, said somebody consolingly, You will have plenty of
time to get distinctions, as you are going to stay on at scholl.

But I might have got a distinction...

Thus sadly he took his leave of the house where he was boarding
at that time, the thought of the lost distincion filling all his
little being, which was already beginning to reveal its latent
greatness».

The weekly review concludes:

«So here was Salazar giving proofs of his extraordinary qualities even
in these little ways. He was upright both physically and morally:
his conduct was irreproachable in youth as in later life. Straightfor-
ward as all men ought to be, for the honour of their species».

＊

＊　　＊

One afternoon I was at Vimieiro in search of materiäl indispensable
for this study of Salazar's character. It is a quiet spot in delightful surroundings. Besidè the hermitage on the Santa Comba
side of the Ponte Nova, I came across two boys, about twelve
years old, looking after some sheep scattered over the fresh green
hillside. The ensuing dialogue seems to me worth recording, if only
as a curiosity.

I addressed the younger. He confessed that he was still learning his
alphabet.

Do you know who Salazar is?

Of course I do.

Well, what is he? What kind of a man is he?

He hesitated a moment, looked on the ground, and at last replied
gravely:

He is a poet...

74

His companion, who was already finishing his primary instruction.
corrected him:

He is a great figure in our history.

I have given the incident in its actual word.

*

*   *

Salazar's father, António de Oliveira, was born at Vimieiro on Juanary
17th, 1839, and died in that village on September 28th, 1932. His
mother, Dona Maria do Resgate, was born at Santa Comba on
October 23rd, 1845, and died at·Vimieiro on November 17th, 1926.

*

*   *

The registers of the University of Coimbra reveal that Salazar obtained in the various subjects of his course — 16 marks once; 17 marks
twice; 18 marks five times; 19 marks ten times.

*

*   *

Between the months of August and September, 1927, Salazar was in
Paris on his way to Liège where, together with Dr Gonçalves
Cerejeira and Dr Alberto Diniz da Fonseca, he attended a con-
gress of Catholic Working Youth.

He was no longer to find in Belgium the gracious figure of Cardinal
Mercier, that great citizen of the world. The International Union
of Social Studies was still continuing, however, and the «Social
Code» was to bear the impress of the tenacious and energetic
spirit of the author of the famous *Course of Philosophy*.

75

A journalist's note.

As representative for the *Diário de Notícias*, my first interview with
the Minister of Finances, Dr Oliveira Salazar, was in the first
or second week of his taking office in 1928. He had doubtless
been giving me some general indications of his projected financial
policy, and I mentioned that ancienty bogey which had so often
conditioned the political action of governments in our country —
I mean, «public opinion».

Salazar promptly took me up.

«Public opinion, no. Rather public conscience. It is of course quite a
different thing, but I pay more heed to it, and rightly.»

In one of the chapters of this book, I have said: «He read La Science
Sociale...» The doctrine of the sociologists Le Play and Edmund
Demolins, authors respectively of «L'organisation du Travail» and
of «La Méthode Sociale», must have assisted Salazar to arrive at
the concept that political régimes are variable according to the
circumstances of time and place. The idea that no political theory
can be put into practice in exactly the same way at all times
and in all countries took firm possession of his mind. At the same
time, he was convinced that there are certain fundamental principles common to all forms of government, however contrary in
spirit. In an interview granted to Frédéric Lefèvre, Salazar
referred to Maurras as an exponent of the theory of «necessary
authority and the strong State». These two schools of French
sociology — *La Science Sociale* on the one hand and this particular
aspect of Maurras on the other — toned each other down suffi-

76

ciently to allow them both a share of influence in the shaping of Salazar's political thought. He pointed out, however, the fallacy in Maurras' principle of *politique d'abord*, but added that it had assisted him to correct in his own thought the opposite extreme of *La Science Sociale*, which did not give sufficient importance to the political factor.

Salazar's conception of government for the Nation would of course be different and original — «a creation which is Portuguese in structure». «Certainly, no foreign experiment, no practical achievement in whatever quarter of the world must be neglected in our desire to gain useful lessons therefrom. But our chief source of instruction, the inspiration of the main outlines of our poltical structure, has been our own history, our traditions and temperament, in short *the Portuguese reality*. (Speech of March 22, 1938).

*

*   *

In these pages I have spoken more than once of Salazar's culture. It is interesting to note that «his studies bear the stamp of Thomism and classical culture which he believes to be indispensable to all true culture». The essential for man, in his opinion, is to be able to think well, since we cannot know everything. «True culture does not seek to furnish the mind, but rather to shape it, to teach it to observe accurately the problems that arise and to extract from them all the lessons they contain. The essential is not to know things, but to know how to reason about them».

I write the closing lines of this short study on the 13th day of May, 1938. The prayers of hundreds of thousands of Portuguese gathered together in the Cova da Iria to give thanks to God for the happy tranquility of our country reecho here in my room, filling it with the sound of voices sweetly singing hymns in praise of Our Lady, «Mother of Portugal»

They are asking God's blessing upon our country and praying for our rulers, upon whom Peace and Work for us all depend. I remember a sentence from The Imitation of Christ: — «Human reason is weak and can be mistaken; but true faith is not deceived».

I unite these lines with the murmured prayers and thanksgivings addressed to Providence watching over us. Like others, I too recognise in Salazar a layman who has preached regeneration to the Portuguese people merely by his own example. It is in the serene assurance of fulfilling a spiritual duty that I have written this book to assist the coming generation towards a perfect understanding of the age from which it springs.

BIBLIOGRAPHICAL NOTES

(1), (2), (3), (4), (5), (6), (7), (8), (9), (11), (12) and (14): «A minha resposta» — António de Oliveira Salazar, 1919; (10) «Quoted in Dois Nacionalismos» — Hipólito Raposo; (13) «Sistema Corporativo» — Marcelo Caetano, 1938; (15) «Anastácio da Cunha» (preface) — Aquilino Ribeiro; (16) «Centro Católico Português» — Oliveira Salazar, 1922; (17) «Salazar — António Ferro; (18) António Sardinha; (19) Act of the 2nd session of the Congress of the Commercial and Industrial Associations of Portugal. Dr. Armindo Monteiro's paper, «A questão do equilíbrio orçamentário», was also discussed at this Congress. Speech by Dr. Levy Marques da Costa; (20) From the book «Eu, os políticos e a Nação» — Cunha Leal. All the sentences quoted are from the lecture, «O Exército e a Política», page 173; (21) «A Paz de Cristo na classe operária» — speech by Dr. Oliveira Salazar at Braga on July 4, 1924; (22) «Diário da Madeira»; (23) «Duas Economias» lecture by Dr. Oliveira Salazar at Coimbra in March, 1928; (24) «Discursos» — vol. 2, (preface) — Oliveira Salazar; (25) «Novidades» of April 27th, 1928.

The review, «Estudos», published by the C. A. D. C. (Coimbra) has been consulted; and also vol. I of the Congresso de Coimbra, published by the Associacion Española para el Progresso de las Ciencias — Madrid, 1925.

Date Due